Gaia's Vision Oracle Cards

Doris Diamond ❖ Susan Starr
Photographic Art by Doris Diamond

Schiffer Publishing Ltd
4880 Lower Valley Road • Atglen, PA 19310

Other Schiffer Books on Related Subjects:

Contact Your Spirit Guides. Asandra.
ISBN: 978-0-7643-3719-2

Spiritual Gardens: A Guide to Meditating in Nature. Danijela Kracun & Charles McFadden.
ISBN: 978-0-7643-3731-4

Watercharms: Ocean-Reiki Meditations. Sylvia M. DeSantis.
ISBN: 978-0-7643-3914-1

The Reluctant Empath. Bety Comerford and Steve Wilson.
ISBN: 978-0-7643-4603-3

Copyright © 2016 by Doris Diamond & Susan Starr

All rights reserved. No part of this work may be reproduced or used in any form or by any means—graphic, electronic, or mechanical, including photocopying or information storage and retrieval systems—without written permission from the publisher.

The scanning, uploading, and distribution of this book or any part thereof via the Internet or via any other means without the permission of the publisher is illegal and punishable by law. Please purchase only authorized editions and do not participate in or encourage the electronic piracy of copyrighted materials.
"Schiffer," "Schiffer Publishing, Ltd. & Design," and the "Design of pen and inkwell" are registered trademarks of Schiffer Publishing, Ltd.

Designed by John P. Cheek
Type set in Times New Roman

ISBN: 978-0-7643-5009-2
Printed in China

Published by Schiffer Publishing, Ltd.
4880 Lower Valley Road
Atglen, PA 19310
Phone: (610) 593-1777; Fax: (610) 593-2002
E-mail: Info@schifferbooks.com

For our complete selection of fine books on this and related subjects, please visit our website at www.schifferbooks.com. You may also write for a free catalog.

This book may be purchased from the publisher. Please try your bookstore first.

We are always looking for people to write books on new and related subjects. If you have an idea for a book, please contact us at proposals@schifferbooks.com.

Schiffer Publishing's titles are available at special discounts for bulk purchases for sales promotions or premiums. Special editions, including personalized covers, corporate imprints, and excerpts can be created in large quantities for special needs. For more information, contact the publisher.

Contents

Introduction 4
    How to use *Gaia's Vision Oracle Cards* 4
    Creation of *Gaia's Vision Oracle Cards* 5
Card Messages 6
Appendix 16
    Suggested Questions and Spreads for Visioning 16
    Readings and Spreads 17

Conclusion 22
Acknowledgments 23
About the Authors 24

Introduction

All ancient peoples had an original creation story, one in which the Earth—or Gaia, the name by which we recognize Earth's living spirit—was dreamed into being by the primordial nothingness. Everything that came from this great dreamer had its own dream, its own vision. Every tree, every rock, every mountain, every river, the air, and all creatures down through the ages are dreamers—as are we—and weave their visions throughout time and space. When we are able to dream in harmony with each other and with Gaia—a dream of peace, prosperity, and balance—we are at our best.

Have you ever had a moment—or an hour or a day—when you felt completely at one with your natural surroundings? You were swimming, perhaps, and felt as fluid as the water, part of it. Or you sank your entire body down into the sand and could feel Gaia's coolness at daybreak, or her heat at midday. You felt as one with Mother Earth then; and, in truth, you are always one with her, and have access to her wisdom, strength, and vitality forever.

We hope this deck recreates that feeling, so you can divine messages and guidance that will offer insight into yourself and into life's big and little mysteries.

How to Use *Gaia's Vision Oracle Cards*

There are many ways to see, and each of these cards can become another pair of eyes for you. When your soul needs a lift, pick a card; the cards and messages may inspire you. Or when you have a question, they can become the eyes of the Mother; you'll be able to access her eternal wisdom to guide you.

Divination is the practice of discerning the hidden significance of events using omens, signs, or methods—such as tarot or oracle cards, runes or tea leaves—or systems, such as astrology. What they all share is the use of intuitive perception to gain information from a deeper or larger source. *Gaia's Vision* uses the deeper, profound wisdom of the Earth Mother as the source from which you can draw. By looking deeply into the multiple layers of nature imagery in each card, you can call up that wisdom and discern an answer or outcome for your question that harmonizes with your soul.

To work with the cards, we suggest creating a quiet space for contemplation. You may already have a way of doing this; if not, you might follow the suggestions here. Experiment until you find a way that works for you.

Find a time and place away from noise or traffic, in your home or outdoors. Lighting a candle or burning some incense, if you can safely do so, helps to set the mood. Sit quietly. Close your eyes and focus on your question for a moment. You might want to hold the cards in your hands as you do this. Say your intention or question aloud and choose a card.

Look at the card in different ways. Think of how you dream. There are no instructions; you enter and leave at random points. Don't be deterred by the position of the title—the cards are quite flexible! Hold the card upright; turn it upside down, or on its side. See what you notice. Look at little pieces of the card—a corner, the top or the bottom. Notice shapes, forms, figures…what do they remind you of? What associations can you make? See if the card tells a story. You might try repeating the question again, or journaling about what you see or feel. Use one card or more if you prefer. If you would like a different perspective, the messages in this book offer some possible meanings for each card.

Use the cards as inspiration for prayers, poetry, story or song, for drawing, painting, or sculpting. Use your imagination and get creative!

Creation of *Gaia's Vision Oracle Cards*

Creating the Cards

From author and art creator Doris:

With some creative inspiration from a photography class I was taking, I began to experiment with combining two of my nature photographs to create a new image. Sometimes the result pleased me more than either of the images alone. The dreamy, mystical quality spoke deeply to me. I showed a few to some friends, and they began to see things in the images that I had not noticed—a bird, wings, the shape of a hand, or a head, etc. How fascinating that people were finding meaning in the photos I was taking! I continued creating more of the images from the thousands of photographs that I had amassed. I followed my intuition to select photographs that would work well together. Oftentimes, the results ended up in the trash bin of my computer, and other times, like magic, they worked!

Creating the Messages

From author Susan:

After Doris created each card, we called our community together for two gatherings, where the vision cards were given out and guests were asked to describe words and feelings that came to mind. We used their feedback as a starting point to name each card. As I kept the guests' words and feelings in my heart, I looked deeply into the layers of the vision card to find the message most evocative of the image. I wrote each of these messages outdoors, where I could feel Gaia's presence in the wind, the ground, and the trees. I used what bubbled up from her vision to blend with the vision cards, which Doris and I later refined into the messages you will find in this book.

Card Messages

Ageless Answers

Cool vortex of intuition forever surrounding you…mossy velvet of memory…soft carpet of experience. You dip in, seeking guidance. The right answer rises up.

Keyword: Wisdom

Birthfire

Possibilities take shape, dissolve… appear anew. Thoughts aflame… quick, playful, deliberate…One ignites, bursting from your center. What will emerge?

Keyword: Creativity

Ancient Light

Sparkling night…you look up, through time. Ancestor spirits live…they stand, tall as trees… speaking truth. Hidden meanings revealed…answers emerge from darkness. A million eternal stars… you dream of the mystery. You know it all within.

Keyword: Timelessness

Budding Heart

Delicate wonder…centered in your core. Bliss and calm…the power to see now what you missed before. Your heart is the gathering place…fresh light dances around your awareness. Beginnings…you are ripe for the secret.

Keyword: Innocence

Center Point

Calm luminescence radiates from your core. Stillness prevails…you see clearly your own lotus soul, the deep peace within. Sit inside it…be open…know joy.

Keyword: Serenity

Cosmic Merge

A bud blooms in night violet… cloudshine defines her edges. You dream, joining Earth and sky, dancing as lovers. Open your eyes now…the dawn of a new light is bright within you.

Keyword: Awakening

Coming Alive

Pink heart petals dance in the light…you are aflutter. Your bubbly soul delights in every movement, every moment. Sweet warmth rises within you…your senses awaken with thanksgiving.

Keyword: Joy

Creative Disarray

Jumbled feelings, details blurred. You swirl in the morass…here decay, there growth…what comes next? No way to know, you are carried by chance. Storms rise…you are falling. Your soul cries out to the universe…it knows…you land on a perfect leaf.

Keyword: Chaos

Dancing the Spiral

At the very core, everything begins…you are the radiant center point…the pulsing purple heart of all. You swirl out, sprinkling starlight in a velvet circle…now forward, now back. Past, present, future all at once…infinite potential, step by step. The divine dance unfurls, within and without…you are the sacred dancer, choosing the rhythm as you go.

Keyword: Becoming

Desire in Bloom

You are the red sun bursting…feel your heat rise. Your heart ignites…your soul sparks. Yellow rippling waves…flames without end. You dance, ecstatic in the fire…burning, vital, vibrant. Open to the bloom, blossom and be wild.

Keyword: Passion

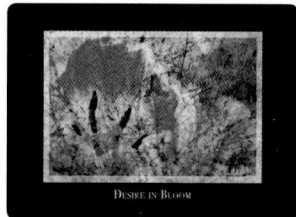

Divine Favor

Waves of calm wash over you…your choices are supported…your beauty is appreciated. Protected and precious, you are beloved. Gaia meets you with a smile.

Keyword: Grace

Diving Deep

Look inside…examine from all angles…you break apart the puzzle. Two sides, at least, to everything…do you see them all? Now is the time to ask before acting.

Keyword: Contemplation

Dreaming Clear

Open-eyed, you imagine…what do you see? Choices…each one a petal leading towards your center. You focus with wisdom. Waypoints illuminated, they guide your way home.

Keyword: Vision

Embracing Spirit

Go into your heart…gently see its nurturing beauty. Touch your true essence…boundless love, glowing aura. You are eternal…unlimited… forever unique.

Keyword: Divinity

Ecstatic Explosion

Wild emotions, sudden release… you are a starseed, emanating light, scattering sound. Your brilliant spirit shines…infusing your world with energy. Pure joy pulses through your blood.

Keyword: Bursting

Eternal All

Energies meld tenderly… enveloping your core with warmth. Hearts embrace…feelings meet, creating a luminous whole. Hidden souls, revealed in raw joy… boundless divinity, revealed in precious earth. You are all that is.

Keyword: Love

Ethereal Bridge

A threshold to something unexplored…soft visions through the rain call you to other dimensions. You take a step… ponder the path…gently anticipate. You wonder where it might lead.

Keyword: Reflection

Flowing Growth

Spinning outward with wild arms, you swirl…a spirit blazing toward massive change. Will delicate details get lost in the frenzy? Like a sea anemone, flowing yet rooted, free to grow.

Keyword: Expansion

Exquisite Plenty

Eternal fullness…you burst with the feeling of enough, savoring life's sweet richness. It's all yours, to have and to share, with love and blessings.

Keyword: Abundance

Gaia's Cord

Spirit walks among the trees…you feel Gaia in the leaves, the roots, the branches. Here and now, time expands…Earth wisdom supports you. The heartbeat of the Mother is steady within you.

Keyword: Grounding

Gentle Embrace

Airy breath of release…sacred space of honoring…know that you are held. Lives connect… where you have been, I have been. Sharing sweet support…friends are everywhere.

Keyword: Compassion

Heartroots

Interwoven with the grove, deep roots anchor your growth. Branches reach ever up, towards the light… ever out, towards nearby hearts. You share space…you share time… you share your lives. Love surfaces and soars.

Keyword: Community

Graceful Yield

Sweet lightness of the purple glen… allowing you to see that which is. Friction is futile here…winds of truth blow through, and serenity comes. Your soul accepts what it sees, and is calm.

Keyword: Surrender

Inner Glow

Vividly bright, you shine from within. Love, confidence, happiness…emotions awake and flowing. Your glow encircles your being…you are made from light, the living starfire. Always remember your brilliance.

Keyword: Radiance

Joyful Body

Succulent flowers surround you… food for body, food for soul…the sweet nectar calls you. Drink deep, replenish yourself. Feed on their beauty…become fresh and alive… grow healthy, strong, and capable.

Keyword: Nourishment

Mists of Tears

You stand in a shimmering waterfall, ready for relief. Warm drops fall…tears flow…pain pours out. Let it go, let it all go…gently releasing, creating space within. Breathe…the veil lifts…treasures of the universe wait for you. Peace washes over you.

Keyword: Cleansing

Lively Waters

You are a stream, a meandering river, an ocean wave…weaving, flowing, bending. Meld mind with spirit …float with the current to your soul's destination. Surrender to intuition.

Keyword: Fluidity

Powerburst

Autumn colors, vibrant and bold… the seed before Gaia's deep sleep. What winter dreams will bloom in your life? Soon, dreamtime ends… wild spring energy plays in your being. You make your musings real.

Keyword: Manifestation

Rainbow Energy

Light floods your dark places, transforming bone and blood… you stand in a cleansing crystal prism. Chakras spin…balance is restored…old wisdom is found again.

Keyword: Healing

Ripe Knowing

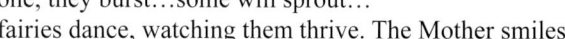

Seed pods spring from the fecund Mother, awaiting their time…so many births are possible. Playful spirits commune…which seeds will bring joy, deep growth? One by one, they burst…some will sprout… fairies dance, watching them thrive. The Mother smiles.

Keyword: Possibility

Regal Strut

Admire your gifts…each an iridescent feather, waiting to be unfurled. Purple richness…power and vision…stand in your beauty. You shine…your heart watches… you know you do it well. Your being radiates confidence. The moment is yours.

Keyword: Pride

Rootwalking

Bare feet in moist soil…send your energy down…plant roots around the ancestors' bones. Roots of other beings, ancient and new, enmesh with yours…the watchers in the woods. They speak to you in one voice…all of creation is with you.

Keyword: Connection

Sacred Belonging

You lift your eyes…the winged ones dance, close enough to touch. Radiant, strong, they encircle you… you are part of this magnificence. Your heart smiles.

Keyword: Reverence

Sparkleburst

Awaken! Your awareness opens to an alternate universe…your fire bursts forth…layers of the ordinary burn away. You are the jewel at the head of a magic wand, spreading light wherever you go.

Keyword: Emergence

Soulful Snapshots

Memories…sharp, hazy, focused… you select the exposure. How will you remember…which will you keep? A teardrop falls…a smile opens wide. Precious are your days.

Keyword: Remembrance

Spirit Signals

Attention, drawn to an unexpected place…the smallest detail fascinates you. What was unseen is now visible…what was unfelt is now visceral. Curiosity ignites your soul…questions burst like red-soaked spring buds. Their first stirrings tingle your heart. You want to know more.

Keyword: Noticing

Thanksblooming

Sweet life, expanding your heart. You grow in harmony with Gaia… every breath pulls you closer to her eternal heart. Smell, touch, taste, hear…see every detail. "Thank you" is your deepest prayer.

Keyword: Gratitude

Visioning Point

Suspended in not-knowing, you wait…different lives call back from the future. One green, verdant… one clear, crystalline…one yet un-imagined, meeting at the now, the source of power. No wrong choice…no right choice…only your choice, felt deep in your belly.

Keyword: Choice

True Being

Turbulent water washes over gray rocks…what's underneath? Shadows dance…your old stories play…they are swept away in the flow. You emerge…crystal bright, shining. Currents of clarity support you now.

Keyword: Transformation

Walking the Path

A soft path through sun-dappled leaves, crimson and green, each step a watercolor dream…create the path as you go. You are passing from your now into your future. Clear the way to joy, notice beauty in each step…breathe in the colors of the heart chakra, and live there. You are the dreamer and the dream.

Keyword: Journey

Appendix

Suggested Questions for Visioning

This deck has been designed so that it will help you answer any question arising from your soul, or to envision what you want to manifest. We've suggested some questions here for those times you may not know exactly where to start or what to ask. You can pick one question or combine several questions into your own spread.

- What is *now* calling me to pay attention?
- What am I grateful for?
- What gift will today bring?
- How can I find more passion in my life?
- How can I be more available to life's moments?
- Where do I feel expansion in my life? Where do I feel contracted or small?
- How can I create more community in my life?
- What challenges might face me today?
- What would enliven my relationships?
- How can I bring more meaning to my life?
- How can I recognize opportunity today?
- What do I notice about the things I remember? Why do I remember them?
- We can think of dreams planted in the consciousness like seeds planted in Gaia's rich soil. What dreams of mine are awakening?
- Where in my life might I be stuck in the grip of old patterns?
- What might more freedom look like for me: a bird spreading its wings, a great river flowing to the ocean?
- What do my senses tell me about what I notice?
- What secrets am I keeping from myself?
- What is my truth?
- How can I feel more comfortable with self-praise?
- In what ways do I stand tall and proud like a tree, and let others see that?
- How can I react more harmoniously to change?
- What do I need to do to make choices more easily?
- How do I cultivate my sense of wonder?
- What does wisdom mean to me?
- What makes me feel divine?
- What old beliefs are still constricting me? Who could I be without those beliefs?
- What do I need to know to increase abundance in my life?

Readings and Spreads

We also invite you to go deeper into your reading by drawing more than one card. We've created nine sample spreads with themes inspired by Gaia you may want to explore. Look through them, and perhaps one will appeal to you. Position the cards you pick the same way that the diagram shows. That way you will remember which question the card is attached to. For example, place the first card in position number one in the diagram; this card corresponds to question number one in the spread. We have found that saying the question aloud focuses your intention. It's a good idea to make note of what questions you ask and which cards go with a particular question.

Reaching for the Stars Spread

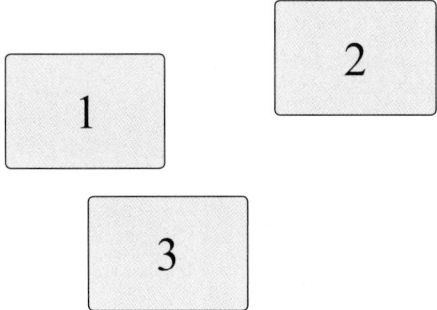

Ask:
1. What dreams have inspired me in the past?
2. What dreams are stirring just below the surface of my consciousness?
3. How can I bring these dreams into reality?

The Wind Spread

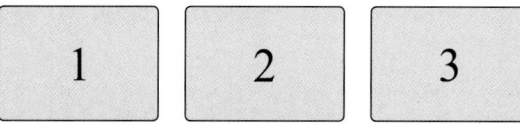

Ask:
1. What old pattern needs to be blown away?
2. How can I release the old pattern?
3. What may come into my life once the old pattern is released?

The Sun Spread

Ask:
1. What inspires me?
2. How can I bring my true self out into the world?
3. What can I offer to the world?
4. What promise can I offer to myself?

The Forest Glen Spread

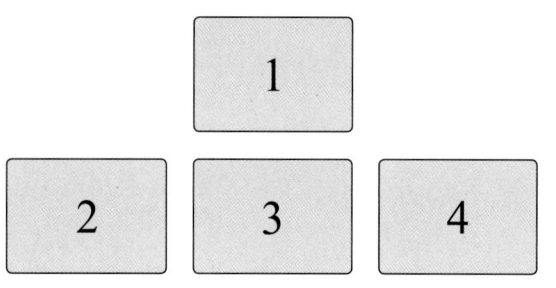

Ask:
1. How do I create a sense of peace in my life?
2. What is one thing that surrounds me as I rest and rejuvenate?
3. What else surrounds me as I rest and rejuvenate?
4. What will come into my life after this period of rest and rejuvenation?

The Mud Spread

Ask:
1. What has been keeping me stuck?
2. What function has that served?
3. How can I move on?
4. What inner strength will help me?

The Moon Spread

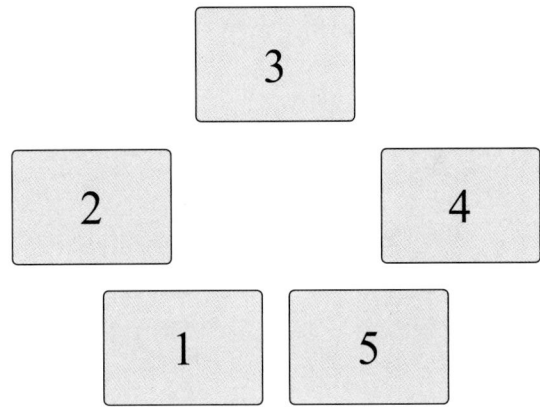

Ask:
1. New moon: what seeds of inspiration are waiting to be nurtured?
2. Waxing moon: what should I remember as these seeds grow?
3. Full moon: what does the light of the full moon clarify?
4. Waning moon: how does what I have learned through this moon cycle become a source of wisdom for me?
5. Dark moon: what still needs further inner reflection?

The Mountain Spread

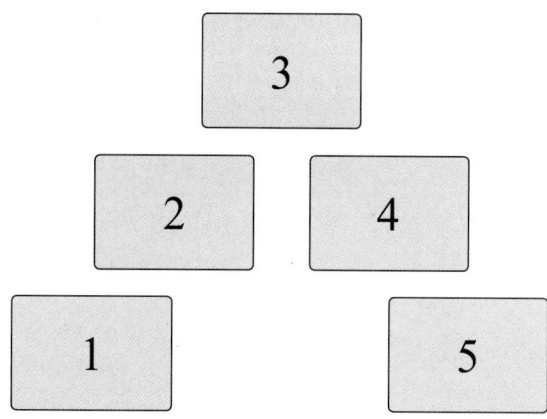

Ask:
1. What is my challenge right now?
2. What will help me work through this challenge?
3. What is waiting for me at the top of the climb?
4. What do I bring back with me after I ascend?
5. How will I have changed after meeting this challenge?

Sacred Fire Spread

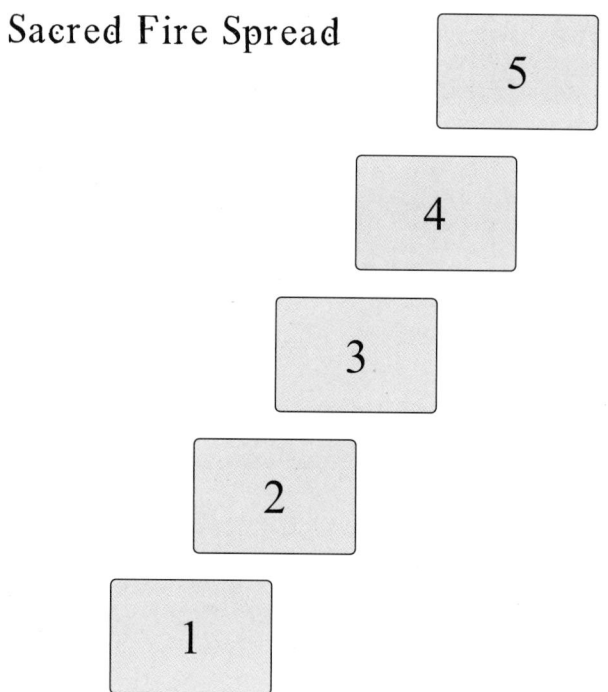

Ask:
1. What is ready to be transformed?
2. What is one step I should take to help this transformation?
3. What is another step I should take to help this transformation?
4. How will spirit help me with this transformation?
5. What gift is waiting for me after this transformation?

The River Spread

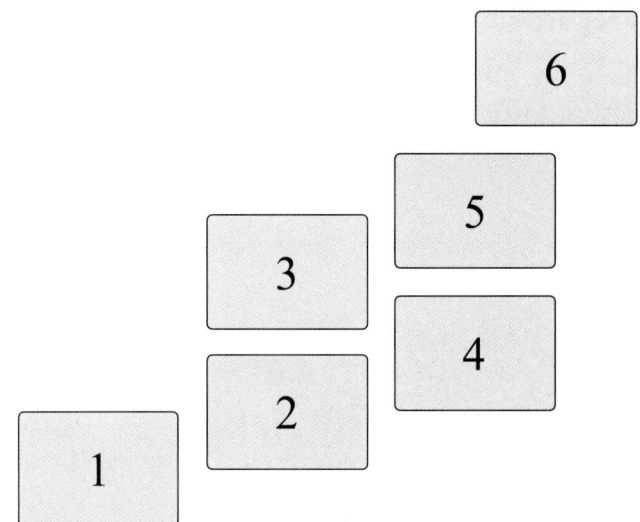

Ask:
1. Where is the current taking me now?
2. What is one challenge that lies ahead?
3. What is another challenge that lies ahead?
4. What is one opportunity that lies ahead?
5. What is a second opportunity that lies ahead?
6. How can I best navigate these challenges and opportunities?

Conclusion

We hope Gaia's Vision will inspire you, excite you, comfort you, and help you birth a vision for a harmonious and joyful life. Thank you for choosing to make the cards part of your journey.

Acknowledgments

We would like to thank Schiffer Publishing marketing team member Chris McClure, who discovered Doris and her work at the Reader's Studio in New York; Dinah Roseberry, our editor at Schiffer, whose encouragement and wit made the journey fun; Liz Foy Casey and Paula Klein, for their time and editorial suggestions; and our circles of friends and family, who generously shared their many visions of the cards and gave us abundant support during their creation. We are grateful to all of you!

About the Authors

Doris Diamond discovered the joy of photography after retiring from teaching elementary school. She has taught numerous workshops about tarot and divination, personal growth and Earth-honoring spirituality. Doris loves to be in nature and to travel the world with a camera in her hands. She is so glad to be on this adventure called life and sharing it enthusiastically with her husband, family, and friends. For more of Doris Diamond's art, please visit www.dorisdiamondimages.com.

Susan Starr is a creative writer, editor, reiki practitioner, and certified holistic health coach. She has been a student of tarot and other divinatory methods for the last dozen years. Nature-based spirituality informs her world view and her connection to the divine. She is a lover of words, of animals, of food, of handmade anything, and of her daughters, most of all. For more information about Susan Starr, please visit www.susanstarr.net.

For more information about Gaia's Vision Oracle Cards, please visit www.gaiasvisionoraclecards.com